THE ULTIMATE 10 Entertainment

VIDEO GAMES

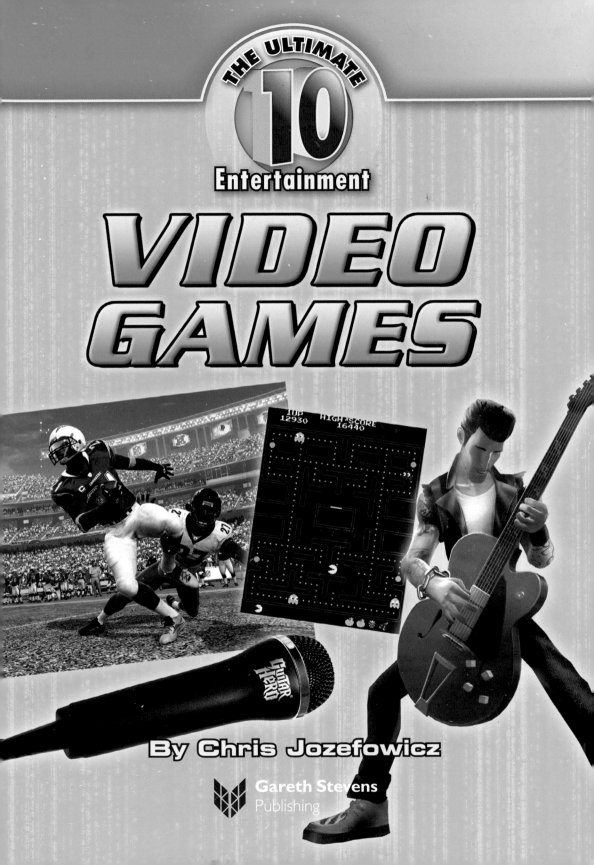

1UP 12930   HIGH SCORE 16440

By Chris Jozefowicz

Gareth Stevens
Publishing

Please visit our web site at www.garethstevens.com.
For a free catalog describing Gareth Stevens Publishing's list of high-quality books, call 1-800-542-2595 (USA) or 1-800-387-3178 (Canada). Gareth Stevens Publishing's fax: 1-877-542-2596

Library of Congress Cataloging-in-Publication Data
Jozefowicz, Chris
   Video games / by Chris Jozefowicz.
       p. cm. — (The ultimate 10: entertainment)
   Includes bibliographical references and index.
   ISBN-10: 0-8368-9167-8   ISBN-13: 978-0-8368-9167-6 (lib. bdg.)
   ISBN-10: 1-4339-2215-0   ISBN-13: 978-1-4339-2215-2 (soft cover)
   1. Video games—Juvenile literature. I. Title.
   GV1469.3.J69 2010
   794.8—dc22   2009008289

This edition first published in 2010 by
Gareth Stevens Publishing
A Weekly Reader® Company
1 Reader's Digest Road
Pleasantville, NY 10570-7000 USA

Copyright © 2010 by Gareth Stevens, Inc.

Executive Managing Editor: Lisa M. Herrington
Senior Designer: Keith Plechaty

Produced by Editorial Directions, Inc.

Art Direction and Page Production: The Design Lab

Picture credits
Key: t = top, c = center, b = bottom, r = right, l = left, (bg) = background
Cover, title page: (l) EA Sports, (c) PAC-MAN® ©1980 NAMCO BANDAI Games Inc., Courtesy of NAMCO BANDAI Games America Inc., (r) Activision, (b) Activision, (bg) Lukiyanova Natalia, used under license from Shutterstock, Inc.; p. 4-5: Yuri Arcurs, used under license from Shutterstock, Inc.; p. 7: PAC-MAN® ©1980 NAMCO BANDAI Games Inc., Courtesy of NAMCO BANDAI Games America Inc.; p. 8: PAC-MAN® ©1980 NAMCO BANDAI Games Inc., Courtesy of NAMCO BANDAI Games America Inc.; p. 9: PAC-MAN® CHAMPIONSHIP EDITION ©1980-2008 NAMCO BANDAI Games Inc., Courtesy of NAMCO BANDAI Games America Inc.; p. 12: (b) ©Fred Prouser/Reuters/ Corbis; p. 13: (b) Press Association via AP Images; p. 15: (t) ©Matthew McVay/Corbis, (b) Tetris NES and Tetris Blockout images provided courtesy of Blue Planet Software, Inc.; p. 16: (t) AP Photo/PopCap Games, (b) Tetris NES and Tetris Blockout images provided courtesy of Blue Planet Software, Inc.; p. 17: ©Andrew Hancock/Icon SMI/Icon SMI/Corbis; p. 19: ©David L. Moore - Lifestyle/Alamy; p. 20: (t) ©David L. Moore - Lifestyle/Alamy, (b) ©Alexdoc/ Dreamstime.com; p. 21: John Shearer/WireImage; p. 23: World of Warcraft and Blizzard Entertainment are trademarks or registered trademarks of Blizzard Entertainment, Inc. in the U.S. and/or other countries; p. 24: (t) World of Warcraft and Blizzard Entertainment are trademarks or registered trademarks of Blizzard Entertainment, Inc. in the U.S. and/or other countries, (b) iStockphoto.com/song_mi; p. 25: World of Warcraft and Blizzard Entertainment are trademarks or registered trademarks of Blizzard Entertainment, Inc. in the U.S. and/or other countries; p. 27: ©Electronic Arts, Inc.; p. 28: (t) ©shopics/Alamy, (b) ©Electronic Arts, Inc.; p. 29: ©Darryl Bush/San Francisco Chronicle/Corbis; p. 32: (t) Archives du 7eme Art/Alamy, (b) Getty Images; p. 35: EA Sports; p. 36: (t) EA Sports, (b) AP Photo/Richard Lam, CP; p. 37: AP Photo/Reinhold Matay; p. 39: ©Square Enix. All Rights Reserved. CHARACTER DESIGN: TETSUYA NOMURA; p. 40: (t) ©Square Enix. All Rights Reserved. CHARACTER DESIGN: TETSUYA NOMURA, (b) AP Photo/Brian Kersey; p. 41: ©Reuters/CORBIS; p. 43: (t) Activision, (b) Activision; p. 44-45: Activision; p. 45: Activision; p. 46: (t) ©INTERFOTO/ Alamy, (c) AP Photo, (b) AP Photo/Shizuo Kambayashi

Printed in the United States of America

1 2 3 4 5 6 7 8 9 14 13 12 11 10 09

Please note that some of the games mentioned in this book may not be suitable for young audiences.

TABLE OF CONTENTS

Words in the glossary appear in **bold** type
the first time they are used in the text.

THE ULTIMATE 10 Entertainment

VIDEO GAMES

Welcome to The Ultimate 10! This exciting series highlights the very best from the world of entertainment.

In this book, you'll explore the amazing world of video games. You'll meet some of the creators of famous games. And you'll learn about the history of gaming.

People of all ages enjoy the challenge of a good video game.

Video games have been around for more than 50 years. They began in science labs. Later, they moved on to video arcades and living rooms. The first video games were played on computers as big as rooms. Today, we play games on small handhelds and even our cell phones.

This book tells the story of 10 ultimate games. They changed the way people play games. They changed how our culture views games. They also provided countless hours of fun to gamers around the world.

Game On!

Here are 10 of the most amazing video games.

#1 Pac-Man

#2 Super Mario Bros.

#3 Tetris

#4 Wii Sports

#5 World of Warcraft

#6 The Sims

#7 GoldenEye 007

#8 Madden NFL

#9 Final Fantasy VII

#10 Guitar Hero

#1

Pac-Man
Leader of the Pac

In the late 1970s, most arcade games had space themes. Toru Iwatani, a young Japanese video game designer, was tired of space battles. He wanted to make a game based on eating, and *Pac-Man* was born. It became the most popular arcade game of all time. Then Pac-Man broke out of the arcades. He chomped his way into homes and became a pop culture legend.

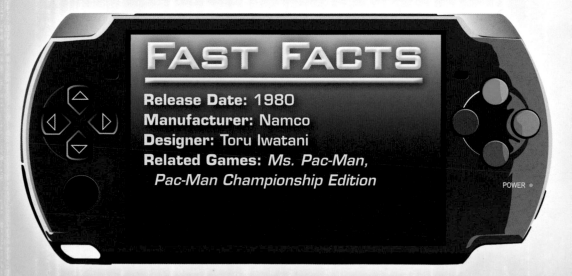

FAST FACTS

Release Date: 1980
Manufacturer: Namco
Designer: Toru Iwatani
Related Games: *Ms. Pac-Man, Pac-Man Championship Edition*

POWER

Each maze has four power pellets.

Each ghost has a nickname. Blinky is red, Pinky is pink, Inky is blue, and Clyde is orange.

Puzzling Players

Pac-Man was first released in Japan in 1980. Arcade fans didn't know what to think of it. Unlike most games, *Pac-Man* had no fighting. Players guided Pac-Man around a maze. He ate pellets and ran from four colorful ghosts. When Pac-Man ate a power pellet, he could then turn around and eat the ghosts.

Break Out

American gamers were looking for new kinds of games. *Pac-Man* was also released in U.S. arcades in 1980. It

"Pac-Man came about as I was having pizza for lunch. I took one wedge and there it was, the figure of Pac-Man."
—Toru Iwatani, creator of *Pac-Man*

became an instant hit. Kids loved the simple action of moving through a maze. Parents liked that the game was not violent. Fans of all ages loved the game's challenge of clearing all the pellets from a maze.

Pac-Man Power

People lined up in arcades to play *Pac-Man*. The munching mouth became the most popular video game character ever. Soon, fans could buy Pac-Man clothes. They could watch Pac-Man cartoons on TV and eat Pac-Man cereal. In 1982, the song "Pac-Man Fever" became a hit.

The popularity of *Pac-Man* led to many **sequels**. *Ms. Pac-Man* became almost as big a hit as *Pac-Man*. Soon, fans could also play *Super Pac-Man*, *Jr. Pac-Man*, and *Pac-Land*.

Pac-Man started in arcade games. The character became so popular he appeared on many products, including sports drinks.

FOR THE RECORD

Intelligent Ghosts

Computer programs called **artificial intelligence (AI)** control how video game characters act. The AI in *Pac-Man* was fairly simple. Players found patterns in how the ghosts behaved. This allowed the players to survive many levels. The ghosts in later *Pac-Man* games had random movements built in. Players couldn't be sure what a ghost would do. This made the games more challenging.

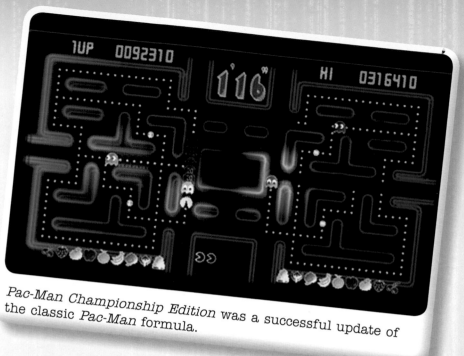

Pac-Man Championship Edition was a successful update of the classic Pac-Man formula.

Pac-Man Lives On

It wasn't long before *Pac-Man* gobbled his way into homes. He showed up first in 1982 for the Atari 2600. *Pac-Man* games continue to be made for computers, games consoles, and handhelds.

Iwatani, *Pac-Man*'s creator, did not work on most of these games. He did, however, create a new *Pac-Man* for the Xbox 360 in 2007. The game, *Pac-Man Championship Edition*, got rave reviews. Simple Pac-Man remains one of the most popular game characters of all time.

DID YOU KNOW?

Pac-Man was originally named *Puck-Man*. When Iwatani created the game, he used a Japanese term for "chewing." In Japanese, *paku-paku* means "chomp-chomp." Iwatani changed *paku* to *puck* and called his game *Puck-Man*. The name was changed to *Pac-Man* when it was released in North America.

#2 Super Mario Bros.
Mr. Video Game

He is an unlikely hero. He's short, he's a bit chubby, and he loves to eat. In earlier years, kids had cowboys and knights as heroes. Now, they have a plumber. We're talking about Mario, of course. He became famous as the star of *Super Mario Bros*. This game set the standard for run-and-jump gameplay. Mario is now the star of a video game empire.

FAST FACTS

Release Date: 1985
Manufacturer: Nintendo
Designers: Shigeru Miyamoto, Hiroshi Yamauchi, Takashi Tezuka
Related Games: *Super Mario World, Super Mario Galaxy*

POWER •

Super Mario Bros. was the most popular game on the Nintendo Entertainment System.

Starting Small

Mario first appeared in arcade games in 1981. He was the hero in *Donkey Kong*. He and his brother Luigi were a hit in *Mario Bros.* The game that made Mario a superstar, however, is *Super Mario Bros.* In the earlier games, Mario appeared on just one screen. In *Super Mario Bros.*, he runs wild across many screens.

Run and Jump

Super Mario Bros. was the first great **platform game**. In a platform game, characters move through a world filled with obstacles. Gamers guide Mario through pipes. He goes over hills and into castles. He fights enemies. Sometimes he stomps on them, and sometimes he hits them with a fireball. The game doesn't make much sense, but players have never had more fun.

> **❝Nintendo's Mario is the elder statesman of the gaming industry.❞**
> —Steven Kent, author of *The Ultimate History of Video Games*

Age of Exploration

Super Mario Bros. helped change what gamers wanted. In arcades, many people played games to get a high score. Mario fans often just liked to explore. Mario's Mushroom Kingdom was colorful. Players could gain power by looking for hard-to-reach areas.

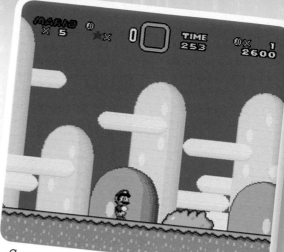

Super Mario World is one of the many sequels to the original Mario game.

Super Mario Bros. led to several sequels. Mario's popularity soon spilled out of video games. Mario maniacs could eat Mario cereal. They watched Mario cartoons and movies. According to one poll, by 1990, more children recognized Mario than Mickey Mouse.

FOR THE RECORD

Meet Mario's Maker
Shigeru Miyamoto is a hero in the world of video games. He works as a game designer at Nintendo. He has helped make games that fans will never forget. He shaped classics such as the Mario games and *The Legend of Zelda*. He also headed the Wii design team. He has been called the Walt Disney of video games. Like Disney, he has created amazing worlds.

Super Mario 64, was one of the first games to let players explore a fully **three-dimensional (3-D)** world.

Mario Magic

Super Mario Bros. was released in 1985. It was a dark time for video games in the United States because fewer people were playing them. *Super Mario Bros.* helped make video games popular again.

The Mario magic has continued to evolve. Mario still has platforming adventures. Now he is also a star of other best-selling games. He is in sports games, **role-playing games (RPGs)**, and racing games. Who would have expected so much from a little plumber?

DID YOU KNOW?

Graphics were pretty simple when Mario was developed. That affected his look. Mario wears a hat because it was hard to show hair moving. A moustache was also easier to show than a mouth.

#3
Tetris
Puzzle Master

How do you rate a game's popularity? One measure is the number of places you can play it. By this measure, *Tetris* is the most popular game ever. Most computers have a version of *Tetris*. So do many cell phones. Millions of people have enjoyed this simple game. Born in Russia, it went on to conquer the world.

FAST FACTS

Release Date: 1985
Manufacturers: Various
Designer: Alexey Pajitnov
Related Games: *Tetris (NES)*,
   Tetris DS

POWER

A Surprise Out of Russia

Russia was not known for video games. A computer programmer named Alexey Pajitnov changed that. He created a puzzle game that became a classic. In *Tetris*, players arrange falling blocks. The blocks are made of four squares, which fit together like puzzle pieces.

Pajitnov's game caused a sensation in Russia in 1985. Over the next five years, it spread around the world. The game was a hit on home computers and home consoles, such as the Nintendo Entertainment System. People of all ages enjoyed the game.

Alexey Pajitnov poses with his creation. *Tetris* (inset photo) is possibly the most popular video game of all time.

> **"A lot of the people at Nintendo are playing the game during their lunch breaks or even when they should be working."**
>
> —Henk Rogers, game designer and the man who brought *Tetris* to Nintendo

King of Casual

Tetris soon became even more popular. It was released for the first Nintendo Game Boy in 1989. The Game Boy was Nintendo's first handheld game system. Tetris was perfect for people on the go. Players could start a new game quickly. They could play for as long as they needed.

Bejeweled Twist is a popular casual game that was released in 2008. The goal is to create a chain of jewels.

People in the video game industry call games like *Tetris* **casual games**. The games are designed for people looking for a little distraction. Casual games have simple controls and simple rules. The best ones, like *Tetris*, are **addictive**. Today, casual games such as *Bejeweled* and *Peggle* are popular.

FOR THE RECORD

The Tetris Trance

Tetris players often find that they can't shake thoughts of the game. They call it the "*Tetris* effect." Some people see *Tetris* shapes in the world around them. Other people dream about *Tetris*. Scientists have studied some *Tetris* players who have lost their memory. They don't remember playing the game, but they remember the falling blocks!

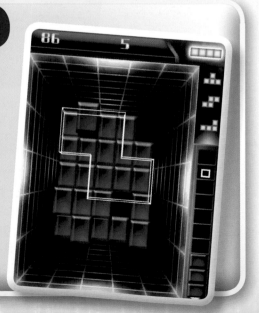

Students dressed as the video game *Tetris* cheer on their team during a college basketball game.

World Domination

The number of versions of *Tetris* is almost uncountable. Game makers have developed many variants of *Tetris*. Some have made three-dimensional (3-D) versions. Nintendo developed *Tetris DS*. This game includes items that can block the progress of players going head-to-head.

Tetris puzzle pieces, or Tetriminos, have become distinctive symbols of *Tetris* in the video game world. They have been used in ads and sculptures. Groups of college students have done projects in which they played *Tetris* on buildings. They use computers to control lights in the windows of tall buildings. The lights make the shapes of falling *Tetris* blocks. *Tetris* is truly the biggest video game of all time!

DID YOU KNOW?

The name *Tetris* combines the prefix *tetra-* and the word *tennis*. *Tetra* means "four" in Greek. The blocks in the game are made of four squares. Tennis is game designer Alexey Pajitnov's favorite sport.

#4

Wii Sports
The Sporting Life

Until recently, couch potatoes could become champions at sports video games. In 2006, Nintendo changed that when it released *Wii Sports*. With *Wii Sports*, players have to get physical. The Wii challenges both new players and experienced gamers.

FAST FACTS

Release Date: 2006
Manufacturer: Nintendo
Designers: Keizo Ohta, Takayuki Shimamura, Yoshikazu Yamashita
Related Games: *Wii Play* (2006), *Wii Fit* (2007), *Wii Sports Resort* (2009)

POWER

Take a Swing

Wii Sports is the first game many people play on the Nintendo Wii. The game features tennis, baseball, bowling, golf, and boxing. These sports use simple motions like swinging and hitting.

Get Physical

The Wii controller was revolutionary. Players no longer controlled the game only by pressing buttons and moving a joystick. The Wii lets them guide the action on-screen by swinging their arms, throwing, and punching. The controls are easy to learn. Gamers feel as if they are playing real sports.

A player gets ready to bat in *Wii Baseball*.

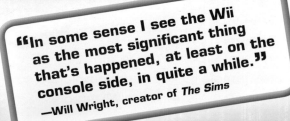

"In some sense I see the Wii as the most significant thing that's happened, at least on the console side, in quite a while."

—Will Wright, creator of *The Sims*

Take a Look at Miis

Wii Sports lets players design their own cartoon characters. These characters are called Miis. The Miis are **avatars**, or stand-ins for the player. The Miis appear as the players on the screen.

Fans love seeing themselves in *Wii Sports*. Using Miis, they can box against their friends and brothers and sisters. When creating Miis, players can control how they look. They can choose hairstyles, eye color, and other features. Some gamers make Miis that look like themselves. Others decide to make Miis that look like movie characters or famous people.

Some Miis can look just like the gamers who designed them.

FOR THE RECORD

Smash!
Some TVs got smashed when the Wii was first released. Why? The wrist strap on the Wii remote wasn't strong enough. Some players let go of the remote when they swung, and the strap broke. The result was a flying remote. Nintendo soon sent thicker straps to Wii owners. They also gave away remote jackets. These cushioned covers give players a better grip. The result is fewer flying Wii remotes.

Wii Like to Party

Wii Sports has been a gateway for new video game fans. The simple controls attract many new players. Some people buy Wiis just so they can play *Wii Sports*. The easy controls also make *Wii Sports* a great game for parties. People soon discovered that *Wii Sports* was great exercise. Players move almost as much as they do when playing the actual sports. Nintendo introduced *Wii Fit*, a game that focuses on fitness. This game helps players improve their health through various exercises.

Wii Sports is one of the top-selling video games of all time. It passed *Super Mario Bros.*, the previous record holder. *Wii Sports* has been a strike, a hole in one, a home run, an ace, and a knockout for Nintendo.

Snowboarder Shaun White shows students his snowboarding game on the *Wii Fit*.

DID YOU KNOW?

Wii Sports can make anyone feel like a sports star, but the game is not true to life. Tennis champion Serena Williams played TV host Conan O'Brien in a game of *Wii Sports* tennis. They played on O'Brien's talk show. Surprisingly, O'Brien won.

#5 World of Warcraft
World War

WoW is an MMORPG. Do you understand that sentence? Then you know something about the future of video games. **Massively Multiplayer Online Role Playing Games (MMORPGs) are some of the most popular games around. They connect gamers around the world.** *World of Warcraft (WoW)* is a blockbuster MMORPG. Many players don't want to leave *Warcraft's* fantasy world once they step inside.

FAST FACTS

Release Date: 2004
Manufacturer: Blizzard Entertainment
Designers: Rob Pardo, Jeff Kaplan, Tom Chilton
Related Games: *World of Warcraft: The Burning Crusade, World of Warcraft: Wrath of the Lich King*

POWER

In *World of Warcraft*, players can join either the Alliance or the Horde. Here, a Horde Blood Elf (left) battles an enemy creature.

Massive Multiplayer

Role-playing games used to be a little lonely. Players met plenty of characters in their quests. It was the computer, though, that controlled the characters. In *World of Warcraft*, real people control other characters. All the gamers play at their own computers.

Pay to Play

Warcraft players pay a fee. This allows them to connect to the game world online. Players create characters and send them on quests. They might fight goblins or dragons. Characters become richer and more powerful as they gain experience. To tackle quests, players sometimes team up with other characters controlled by real people.

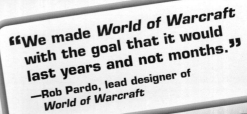

"We made *World of Warcraft* with the goal that it would last years and not months."
—Rob Pardo, lead designer of *World of Warcraft*

Work and Play

Many *World of Warcraft* characters have special professions. Some are traditional sword-fighting heroes. Others have roles that did not exist in earlier role-playing games. Some players become tailors or blacksmiths. They don't do much fighting.

Players can meet many other characters in the *World of Warcraft* game world.

Warcraft players love to meet other players online. Their characters can live together in **virtual** towns. Some players set up virtual weddings for their characters. Players can become completely wrapped up in the game. They spend all their free time playing it.

FOR THE RECORD

Golden Farm

World of Warcraft players want to make stronger, richer characters. Some want it so much that they are willing to pay for it. Thousands of people in the real world are **gold farmers**. They collect gold coins while playing the game. Then they sell the coins to other players in exchange for real money. The players use the coins to buy weapons and other things in the game.

Warcraft World

World of Warcraft is the most popular MMORPG. More than 10 million players around the world subscribe. To keep the game fresh, the game makers keep releasing new levels with new characters.

Many games now allow players to interact in virtual worlds. Not every MMORPG is an adventure game. Games like *Club Penguin* aim for kid gamers. Other games appeal to science-fiction fans. It doesn't matter what the subject is. It just matters that the game world feels almost alive.

The Lich King is the key character on one of the latest versions of *World of Warcraft*.

DID YOU KNOW?

A killer illness once infected *World of Warcraft*. The designers created a spell that took health from a player. The illness passed from player to player. It spread to the whole game world. The game makers had step in to "cure" it.

#6
The Sims
Small World

In the 1980s, Will Wright created a game called *SimCity*. In this game, players build the major functions of a city. After the success of that game, Wright wanted to make a game about real life. His coworkers thought it was a bad idea because they thought no one would want to play it. But Wright proved them wrong. His creation, *The Sims*, became the best-selling computer game of all time.

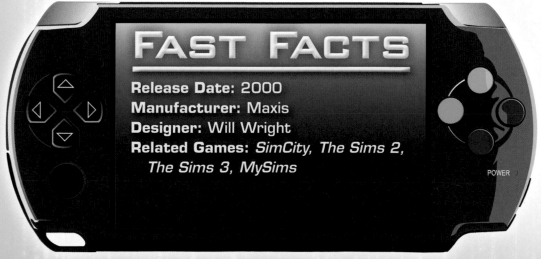

FAST FACTS

Release Date: 2000
Manufacturer: Maxis
Designer: Will Wright
Related Games: *SimCity*, *The Sims 2*,
    The Sims 3, *MySims*

POWER

Players control how their Sims go about their everyday lives.

Attention to Details

Wright's game simulates a person's life. A **simulation** is an imitation of something in real life. *Sims* players control the everyday lives of game characters. The characters eat, exercise, and go to work. Wright's coworkers thought people wouldn't want to play. Don't they have enough chores in their real lives? For game fans, the answer turned out to be a huge no.

Sim-ply Fun

Gamers love acting out fantasies with their characters. The characters are called Sims. Players can help their Sims buy a big house. They can then buy things to put in the house. Players can even find ways to let their Sims fight or die.

> **❝** *The Sims* changed the way people play video games and also changed the kinds of people who play video games. **❞**
> —Bing Gordon of Electronic Arts, publisher of *The Sims*

Little People, Big Success

The Sims became the best-selling home computer game of all time. It soon spawned a sequel, *The Sims 2*, and many expansion packs. The expansions give players more clothes, furniture, and tasks for their Sims. Some expansions let players teach their Sims magic spells. Others let them become famous entertainers.

The Sims attracted players new to video games. For the most part, video game fans have been men. *The Sims*, however, has been popular with women. Close to half of the players now are women.

All video game stores have a wide selection of *Sims* games. *Sims* games have proven very popular among women.

FOR THE RECORD

Do You Speak Simlish?

Sims characters spend a lot of time talking to each other, but they don't speak English. Instead, they speak Simlish. Game designer Will Wright made up the language. The language is nonsense, but it sounds like it could be real. Musicians have recorded songs in Simlish for game soundtracks.

A designer works on the character D. J. Candy from the *MySims* game for the Wii.

Sim Everything

Wright has helped create many other simulation games, including *SimCity*, *SimEarth*, *SimAnt*, *SimCopter*, and *MySims*. In *MySims*, a game developed for the Wii, players move into a run-down town and try to turn it into a lively town.

Wright's games helped popularize life simulation games. Now, gamers regularly care for virtual creatures in games. *The Sims* set the standard for simulating life. Without it, gamers today might not be playing *Nintendogs* and *Viva Piñata*.

DID YOU KNOW?

Modders are people who program their own game content. Some of them love making their own version of *Sims* stuff. The modders make new *Sims* clothes, furniture, and personalities.

#7
GoldenEye OO7
Gun Game

Nintendo games often have a "kiddie" image. The Nintendo 64, however, introduced players to the violent world of the spy James Bond. In *GoldenEye 007*, players take control of James Bond's weapons. As Bond, they shoot their way to victory. *GoldenEye* set the standard for shooting games on home systems.

FAST FACTS

Release Date: 1997
Manufacturer: Rare
Designer: Martin Hollis
Related Games: *Perfect Dark*

POWER

Silenced weapons help *GoldenEye 007* players to sneak their way through missions.

Computer Killer

GoldenEye 007 is a **first-person shooter (FPS)** game. In FPSs, the player sees the world through the eyes of a character holding a gun. Before *GoldenEye*, the best FPSs were played on home computers. Computers have enough power to show good 3-D graphics. Using a mouse also made aiming easier.

Spy Game

The world of FPS changed forever with *GoldenEye 007*. The game has all the action of the James Bond movie *GoldenEye*. The Nintendo 64 had enough power to show good graphics. Players didn't mind using a game controller instead of a mouse. *GoldenEye 007* proved that home systems were ready for FPSs.

> **"Millions of people were introduced to the joys of the FPS by the majestic GoldenEye on the N64."**
> —Stuart Campbell, video game historian and journalist

Choose Your Game

Players love the variety of the action in *GoldenEye 007*. For some levels, they have to sneak carefully. Other levels require huge shoot-outs. In many levels, players can choose their style of fighting.

The multiple player versions on *GoldenEye 007* created a sensation. Four players could compete against one another. One of the most popular multiplayer games is a **deathmatch**. In this type of game, players hunt one another.

GoldenEye 007 is loosely based on the *GoldenEye* movie, starring Pierce Brosnan as James Bond.

FOR THE RECORD

Gaming Goes Major League

Many popular FPS games have copied the *GoldenEye 007* multiplayer formula. It has influenced games such as *Halo* and *Call of Duty*. Competitive multiplayer games have become big business. An organization called Major League Gaming holds tournaments. Top gamers compete for prize money.

Players compete in a Major League Gaming tournament.

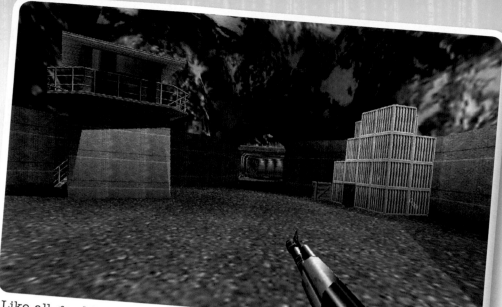

Like all good FPSs, *GoldenEye 007* features a wide variety of weapons for players to use.

Fighting Spirit

GoldenEye 007 became a huge seller for the Nintendo 64. It was followed by a sequel called *Perfect Dark*. Like *GoldenEye*, this game gives players exciting gameplay. Some members of the team who made *GoldenEye* also created a new series of games. Their *TimeSplitters* FPS games have kept the guns blazing.

Today, *GoldenEye 007*'s spirit continues to influence FPS games. The game helped blast shooting games onto consoles. It helped to make FPS one of the most popular forms of action games.

DID YOU KNOW?

GoldenEye 007 is a first-person shooter game. At first, however, it was supposed to be a **rail shooter**. First-person shooters allow players to move where they want. Rail shooters allow players to shoot where they want, but their characters move as if they were riding along rails.

#8

Madden NFL
Fantasy Football

No video game does sequels like *Madden NFL*. Over 20 years, the series has produced more than 20 games. It stays up-to-date with the world of sports. This allows the games to feel true to life. Players enjoyed designing their own plays and creating their own teams. *Madden NFL* has just about perfected the game of virtual football. It is the king of sports video game series.

FAST FACTS

Release Date: 1988
Manufacturer: Electronic Arts (EA) Sports
Designers: Various
Related Games: *NFL Head Coach, NFL Street, NCAA Football 10*

POWER

Minnesota Viking Adrian Peterson avoids a tackle in *Madden NFL*. In the game, players appear incredibly life-like.

Going Pro

John Madden is not the most obvious candidate for sports game fame. He was a football commentator on TV when the game was first released in 1988. Back then, computers were much less powerful. So each team in the first *Madden* game had six players. In real life, teams have 11 players. In 1988, the *Madden* teams and players were fictional. Gamers loved *Madden NFL*, however, because it gave them a lot of options.

Over time, the *Madden* sequels became complex. Eventually, *Madden* football games featured real National Football League (NFL) players. EA Sports makes the *Madden* game. In 2004, the company signed a deal with the NFL. Only *Madden NFL* could use real NFL teams and players.

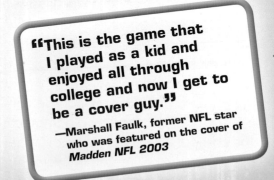

"This is the game that I played as a kid and enjoyed all through college and now I get to be a cover guy."

—Marshall Faulk, former NFL star who was featured on the cover of *Madden NFL 2003*

Madden NFL lets players control real football superstars, such as Tony Romo (9) of the Dallas Cowboys.

Game Changers

Over the years, *Madden NFL* games have continued to evolve. EA Sports releases an update every year. This way, the games keep up with real-life player changes. Rookie players appear in the game. Players who are traded appear on their new teams. Gamers see the real NFL reflected in their game.

EA Sports also tweaked the games for fans. It added new game modes that allowed players to control teams over multiple seasons. Players can also control great NFL teams of the past. The company added different ways to tackle. It even included movement controls for the Wii version of the game.

FOR THE RECORD

Catch and Capture

In 20 years, the graphics of games went from blocky to beautiful. *Madden NFL*, *NBA Live*, and other games use **motion capture** to make sure the characters look real. Motion capture uses the motion of real people. The players wear special outfits that are tracked by a computer. The computer turns the real movement into the game characters' movements.

Reggie Bush (left) of the New Orleans Saints and a fan compete in in the EA Sports Madden NFL '09 championships.

Video Vision

Madden NFL is a best seller in the United States. It is so popular that each year, EA Sports holds a *Madden* competition called the Madden Bowl. Real NFL players compete for a trophy and a featured spot in the next video game.

The influence of *Madden NFL* is changing how fans think about real football. The sports network ESPN recently announced a partnership with EA Sports. The partnership lets commentators at ESPN interact on-screen with virtual players. They can show how plays might work in real life. Life now imitates games like *Madden NFL*.

DID YOU KNOW?

Many football fans believe in the "Madden Curse." Several NFL players who have appeared on the cover of the game package don't play as well afterward. Some have been injured. EA Sports representatives say they don't believe in the curse.

#9

Final Fantasy VII
Great Escape

Some video game worlds are too big to be held in one game. The realm of *Final Fantasy* is such a world. The *Final Fantasy* universe features more than a dozen adventures. The series hit a peak with *Final Fantasy VII*. This role-playing game has an amazing story and beautiful look. Role-playing games have been imitating it ever since it came out.

FAST FACTS

Release Date: 1997
Manufacturer: Square
Director: Yoshinori Kitase
Character Design: Tetsuya Nomura
Related Games: *Final Fantasy X, Final Fantasy XII , Crisis Core: Final Fantasy VII*

POWER

Fantasy Foundations

The *Final Fantasy* series is ancient by video game standards. The first game was released in 1987. Over the years, the game makers crafted a colorful world filled with memorable characters. In it, magic and technology mixed. Players controlled a group of heroes on a role-playing adventure. Characters became more powerful as they explored and fought monsters.

A Match for the Movies

The game consoles that play *Final Fantasy* games also grew more powerful. The series exploded in popularity with the seventh game, which was released for the PlayStation. It had 3-D graphics. It also had vivid music and a complex story. Critics said that *Final Fantasy VII* didn't just imitate the movies. It outdid them.

The popularity of this title led to the creation of the *Compilation of Final Fantasy VII*. This series of games included sequels and **prequels** to *Final Fantasy VII*.

Cloud Strife is the main character in *Final Fantasy VII*.

> **"*Final Fantasy VII* may well be the first 'interactive movie' that's actually enjoyable to play."**
> —Andrew Vestal, game reviewer at gamespot.com

Team Effort

Final Fantasy VII is like a blockbuster movie. It required the work of many people. More than 100 programmers and artists worked on the game. It cost many millions of dollars. Never before had game makers spent so much time on one game. The game had so much detail, it came on three game disks.

Fans of role-playing games loved it. New fans came on board. *Final Fantasy VII* became one of the best-selling games for the PlayStation.

Advent Children is a movie that stars the characters of the *Final Fantasy VII* game.

FOR THE RECORD

More Than Bloops and Bleeps
Final Fantasy VII has a sweeping soundtrack that outdoes many movies. The music is so popular that it has been released on its own. Many other *Final Fantasy* games also have popular soundtracks. In Japan, orchestras sometimes perform the songs in concerts.

Fans in Tokyo stop to try out *Final Fantasy X.*

Role-Playing Planet

The *Final Fantasy* series continues to be a best seller. By 2009, there were 12 games in the main series. Characters from the main series also appear in spin-off games. Comic books are set in the *Final Fantasy* universe. At some fan parties, people dress up like characters from the game.

Final Fantasy VII's popularity changed the landscape of video gaming. Before *Final Fantasy VII*, only a few role-playing games were released a year. Now, a few are released each month.

DID YOU KNOW?

Donald Duck is not your typical role-playing game character. But he is a hero in the *Kingdom Hearts* games, where Disney and *Final Fantasy* characters have adventures alongside one another. Talk about Goofy!

#10
Guitar Hero
Mock Rockers

Video game players sometimes imagine themselves as the heroes of adventures. *Guitar Hero* lets them play heroes onstage. The game has revolutionized music games. It has a unique controller. It has a list of awesome songs. Most important, *Guitar Hero* allows millions of players to live out their rock-and-roll dreams.

FAST FACTS

Release Date: 2005
Manufacturer: RedOctane
Designer: Rob Kay
Related Games: *Guitar Hero® II, Guitar Hero® World Tour, Guitar Hero® III: Legends of Rock, Guitar Hero®: Aerosmith, Guitar Hero®: Metallica*

POWER

The goal of *Guitar Hero World Tour* is the same as the original version. Players try to hit the right notes—and have fun!

Cool Controllers

Video game players could rock out before *Guitar Hero* came along. Arcade games included guitar and drum controllers. Home games like *PaRappa the Rapper* let players use typical game controllers to make music. *Guitar Hero* is the best of both. It has an instrument-shaped controller, and it is played on home game systems.

Rock-and-Roll Fantasy

Guitar Hero players tap buttons in time to music. The controller is much simpler than a real guitar. Still, players feel like they are playing their favorite music. The game uses songs by rock bands such as Red Hot Chili Peppers and Black Sabbath. This has helped make *Guitar Hero* a sensation.

> **"I actually think it's a good thing. I think it introduces kids to music."**
> —Real-life rocker and guitarist Yngwie Malmsteen on *Guitar Hero*

More Music

Guitar Hero has been so successful that it has spawned many sequels and additions. Special song packs are popular. One is nothing but songs from the 1980s. Other sequels have songs by the bands Aerosmith and Metallica. Fans of *Guitar Hero* now have hundreds of songs they can play. Many versions include real songs by the original bands.

Guitar Hero II expanded the number of parts that could be played in a song. It includes a multiplayer mode. A second player can join the band on rhythm guitar or bass guitar.

Guitar Hero World Tour features real songs by real bands. Players choose thier musicians.

FOR THE RECORD

More Fun Than a Radio

The music industry noticed *Guitar Hero*'s popularity. The first game had all cover songs. Those are songs performed by someone other than the original performers. New versions of the game feature songs with the original performances. *Guitar Hero* can help sell music. In the old days, music fans first heard a new song on the radio. Today, bands like Guns 'N' Roses and Smashing Pumpkins release new songs for *Guitar Hero*.

Join the Band

In 2008, a new *Guitar Hero* game made big changes to the series. *Guitar Hero World Tour* added a drum set and a microphone to the classic guitar controller. Now, gamers can form an entire virtual band.

Guitar Hero World Tour also added a feature where gamers can create their own songs from scratch. As the series grows, more and more gamers are picking up their controllers and rocking out.

Up to four players can rock at the same time in *Guitar Hero World Tour*.

DID YOU KNOW?

Teenager Chris Chike loved *Guitar Hero*. He turned his love of the game into a job. Chike holds the record for highest score on *Guitar Hero*. He works as a spokesperson for a company that makes the guitar-shaped controllers.

Pong

Released in arcades in 1972
For home in 1975

Pong was not the first video game, but it was the first video game to become wildly popular. *Pong* consisted of blocks knocking a square ball back and forth. Today, the game looks shockingly simple. In the 1970s, though, it seemed futuristic. It was easy to play, and anyone could join in.

The Legend of Zelda: Ocarina of Time

Released for Nintendo 64 in 1998

A character named Link is Nintendo's adventure hero. *The Legend of Zelda: Ocarina of Time* was Link's first 3-D adventure. Shigeru Miyamoto (left) is one of the award-winning game's designers. He says it pushed the Nintendo 64 to its limits. The game gives players a thrilling adventure in a beautiful world.

Gran Turismo 3

Released for PlayStation 2 in 2001

Some of the earliest arcade games were car-racing games. These games have been improving for more than 30 years. Racing games reached a peak with Sony's *Gran Turismo* series. *Gran Turismo 3* has realistic action and amazing graphics. Other car-racing games are still eating its dust.

Glossary

addictive: causing a person to feel unable to stop doing something

artificial intelligence (AI): computer programs that carry out tasks that normally require human intelligence

avatars: stand-ins for a player in a game

casual games: video games with simple rules that are easy to play

deathmatch: a multiplayer game in which players hunt each other

first-person shooter (FPS): a type of video game in which players carry a gun and see the world through a character's eyes

gold farmers: people who earn experience points or money in a game and sell it to another player in the real world

graphics: images that appear on a video game screen

Massively Multiplayer Online Role Playing Games (MMORPGs): role-playing games that large groups of people play together online

motion capture: a technique that translates people's movements into computer graphics

platform game: a type of game in which players make a character run and jump through a world that is like an obstacle course

prequels: games that were created later but tell the stories before earlier games

rail shooter: a game that guides players along a course while players control where they aim

role-playing games (RPGs): games in which characters evolve and become stronger as they experience adventures and fights

sequels: games that continue or are related to earlier games

simulation: an imitation of something in real life

three-dimensional (3-D): having or appearing to have height, length, and depth, like objects in the real world

virtual: seeming to exist because a computer program creates it

For More Information

Books

Burnham, Van. *Supercade: A Visual History of the Videogame Age 1971–1984*. Cambridge, MA: MIT Press, 2003.

Guinness World Records. *Guinness World Records Gamer's Edition*. New York: Time Inc. Home Entertainment, 2008.

Kent, Steven. *The Ultimate History of Video Games*. New York: Three Rivers Press, 2001.

Web Sites

Moby Games: New Reviews, Game Updates, New Screenshots, and MobyRank Updates
www.mobygames.com
Keep up with latest video games and reviews.

PBS: The Video Game Revolution
www.pbs.org/kcts/videogamerevolution/index.html
Read about the history of video games.

Index

About the Author

Chris Jozefowicz studied to be a scientist but ended up a writer. He has written scientific papers, medical reports, news stories, magazine articles, and video game reviews. He lives in Louisville, Kentucky, with his wife and daughter. He thanks all the game makers whose work has entertained him since he got his first Atari in 1980.